W9-CDP-405

I WAS THERE

PYRAMIDS

OF ANCIENT EGYPT

I WAS THERE

PYRAMIDS
OF ANCIENT EGYPT

JOHN D. CLARE

Consultant Editor ROSALIE DAVID

RIVERSWIFT

LONDON

First published in Great Britain in 1991 and reprinted 1992, 1993, 1994 by The Bodley Head Children's Books. This edition published 1994 by Riverswift, Random House, 20 Vauxhall Bridge Road, London SW1V 2SA.

Random House Australia (Pty) Ltd
20 Alfred Street, Sydney, NSW 2061, Australia

Random House New Zealand Ltd
18 Poland Road, Glenfield, Auckland 10, New Zealand

Random House South Africa (Pty) Ltd
PO Box 337, Bergvlei 2012, South Africa

Copyright © 1991 Random House UK Limited
Text copyright © 1994 John D. Clare
Photographs copyright © 1991 Charles Best

John D. Clare and Charles Best have asserted their right to be identified respectively as author and photographer of this work.

All rights reserved

ISBN 1 898304 72 6

A CIP catalogue record for this book is available from the British Library.

Photography Charles Best
Director Tymn Lintell
Production Manager, Photography Fiona Nicholson
Designer Dalia Hartman
Visualization/Systems Operator Antony Parks
Editor Gilly Abrahams
Editorial Assistant Valerie Tongue
Map and time-line Simon Ray-Hills
Typesetting Sue Estermann
Reproduction F.E. Burman Ltd, Columbia Offset Ltd, Dalim Computer Graphic Systems U.K. Ltd, J. Film Process Ltd, Scantrans, Trademasters Ltd.

Printed and bound in China

ACKNOWLEDGEMENTS

Advisers: The British Museum, Department of Egyptian Antiquities. Costumes: Joanna Measure, Val Metheringham. Jewellery: Angi Woodcock. Make-up: Alex Cawdron, Caroline Kelly, Pat Postle, Hilary Steinberg. Model-makers: Richard Johnston, Chris Lovell, Neville Smith. Props: Caroline Gardener, Helen Pettit. Casting and movement consultant: Mike Loades assisted by Gordon Summers. Photographer's assistant: Alex Rhodes. Picture research: Valerie Tongue.

Additional photographs: Reproduced by courtesy of the Trustees of the British Museum, pp62 bottom right, 63 centre left; Antony Parks pp26-27; Robin Scagell pp30-1; Spectrum Colour Library, pp8-9, 42-43, 48-9; Zefa Picture Library, pp1-5, 6-7, 40-1.

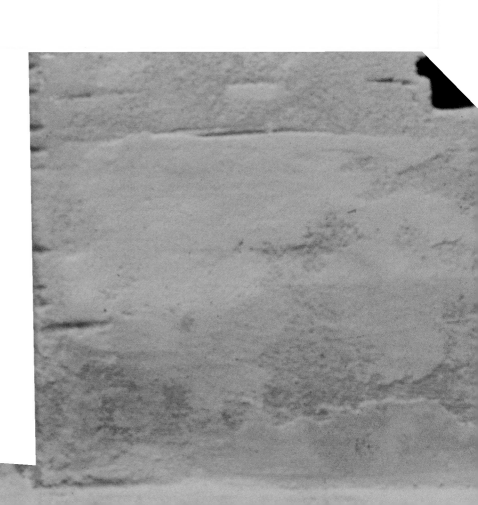

Contents

Ancient Egypt

Around 4,500 years ago, when people in northern Europe were still living in Stone Age huts and eating berries, a flourishing civilization existed in Egypt. The rulers of the time began to build enormous tombs for themselves, called pyramids. The pyramids

at Giza were built 1,200 years before the reign of Tutankhamun and 2,500 years before Queen Cleopatra. They were as ancient to Cleopatra as the ancient Greeks are to us.

The Egyptian civilization grew up along the valley of the River Nile. The southern part of the country, between Aswan and Giza, was known as *Ta-shema* (Upper Egypt). Here the valley is only 12 miles (20 kilometres) across at its widest, and the weather is hot and dry. On either side of the valley there is desert, which the Egyptians called *Deshret* (the Red Land).

Five hundred miles (800 kilometres) north of Aswan the river divides before flowing into the Mediterranean Sea. This delta area was called *Ta-meh* (Lower Egypt). It is a low, flat area of grassland, marshes and refreshing breezes.

There was very little rain in ancient Egypt. What rain there was usually came in torrential, destructive downpours, so the ancient Egyptians regarded rain as a very inferior way of watering the land. All the water for farming and drinking was taken from the River Nile. In addition, it flooded every year and covered the land with a layer of fertile black mud. The ancient Egyptians called their country *Kemet* (the Black Land). The ancient Greeks were the first people to use the name Egypt.

Upper and Lower Egypt were united, in about 3100 BC, by King Menes from Upper Egypt. Menes established his capital on the border between the two countries, where he built the Palace of the White Wall. In later times the Egyptians referred to their ruler as the *Per-aa* (great house), from which comes the modern word pharaoh. Eventually, a town called Memphis grew up around the palace.

Ancient Egypt was divided into about 38 districts called nomes. They had names such as 'Serpent nome', 'Ostrich feather nome' and 'Mummified falcon nome'.

Religion and beliefs

The Egyptians had nine chief gods. Osiris, the god of the dead, was the most popular. They believed that he had been killed by his

brother, the evil god Seth, but was restored to life by Isis, his sister and wife. Nephthys, the protector of the dead, was the sister and wife of Seth. The other gods controlled the natural world. There was Nut, the sky goddess, who stretched out over the earth; Shu, the air god; Geb, the earth god; Tefnut, goddess of moisture; and Re, the sun god. The Egyptians believed that each day Re took the sun across the sky in a boat.

The pharaohs of Egypt, following the example of Seth and Osiris, often married their sisters.

There were many other gods including Khnum, the creator of man; Thoth, the inventor of writing; Ptah, the god of craftsmen; Anubis, the undertaker-god; and Sebek, the crocodile god.

Horus, the falcon, was the protector of Egypt. Egyptians believed that their pharaoh was the god Horus in human form.

Egyptian priests taught that beyond the western horizon lay the subterranean Kingdom of Osiris, the spirit world of the dead. All ordinary Egyptians hoped to go to this land when they died. Above the skies, however, lay heaven, the land of the gods, ruled over by Re. Only the pharaoh, they believed, was pure and powerful enough to go to heaven. When a pharaoh died he was said to have gone up to the horizon.

It was because of their belief in an afterlife that the Egyptians mummified (preserved) their dead, and built the pyramids.

The ruler

The period of Egyptian history from 2686 to 2181 BC is called the Old Kingdom.

In 2558 BC a new pharaoh, Chephren, inherited the throne of Egypt from his father, Cheops.

Chephren was the fourth pharaoh of the fourth dynasty (family of pharaohs). He was the grandson of Seneferu, who had founded

the fourth dynasty. Chephren was married to his sister, Khame-re-nebti, and may have had three other wives as well.

When Chephren was crowned he walked round the Palace of the White Wall, to the south and to the north, to demonstrate his lordship over both Upper and Lower Egypt. He wore two crowns, the red crown of Lower Egypt, and the white crown of Upper Egypt.

Chephren was probably more powerful than any other ruler in Egypt's history. He was the head of the government and the chief priest. His commands could not be questioned, and his word automatically became law. All of Egypt was his private estate. He was the first pharaoh to call himself 'the great god' and 'the son of Re'.

Every two years Chephren travelled through Egypt on a tour known as the following of Horus. Sailing along the Nile on the royal barge, he visited each nome, inspecting the accounts of the local officials. As he travelled, the nobles raised their hands in worship, and cried: 'Adoration to you, O god. Your people can see how beautiful you are.'

The size and magnificence of Chephren's pyramid are an indication of his power and wealth.

The Great Pyramid

The first Egyptian pyramid was built by Pharaoh Zoser in about 2650 BC. During the next ten centuries the rulers of Egypt built about 90 pyramids. The largest and most famous are those at Giza, which were built by Cheops, Chephren and Mycerinus (Chephren's son).

The Great Pyramid of Cheops is the largest stone building in the world. The cathedrals of Florence, Milan, St Peter's in Rome, and St Paul's Cathedral and Westminster Abbey in London could stand together in the area of its base. It was so strongly built that the first archaeologists were able to explore inside by blasting tunnels with gunpowder, without causing it to collapse. Even in the time of the pharaohs rich Egyptians made tourist trips to see it.

Every pyramid was part of a larger complex, including two temples and some-times smaller pyramids, possibly for the queens. Near the Great Pyramid were the smaller mastabas (traditional brick tombs) of important noblemen.

A pyramid was a religious monument. To the Egyptians, its sloping sides represented the rays of the sun god, Re. They believed that the dead pharaoh could climb this way to heaven.

Building a pyramid took much of Egypt's wealth and the labour of thousands of people over a period of 20 or 30 years. It is amazing that the ancient Egyptians expended so much effort to get just one human being to heaven.

Pharaoh Chephren's pyramid is still under construction, but the Great Pyramid, known to the Egyptians as 'the Horizon of Cheops', is finished, and the body of Pharaoh Cheops is buried there. The pyramid stands 481 feet (146 metres) high. Each side measures 756 feet (230 metres). Within it are 2.3 million blocks of stone – enough to build a low wall around the earth. The entrance to the burial chamber is situated high above ground level on the north side of the pyramid. It is completely hidden by casing stones, so that it will remain secret.

The pyramid has been built with great precision. The difference between the longest and the shortest sides is less than 8 inches (20 centimetres). The corners are almost perfect right angles (0.09 per cent error), and the base is almost perfectly flat (0.004 per cent error). The casing stones on the outside of the pyramid are so accurately positioned that it is impossible to push even a hair into the joints.

The Time of Flood

In a good year the Nile flooded 27 feet (8 metres) high at the Palace of the White Wall. In the time of Pharaoh Zoser seven years of low floods caused famine. If the flood was too high the crops failed because the water took too long to subside. Priests used nilometers to measure the flood. Officials were then able to forecast the yield of the harvest and calculate how much tax people would have to pay on their share of the crops.

The river had a great influence on Egyptian civilization. The Egyptians had to channel the

ɔod waters onto the fields, and dam them ɔ that the mud was deposited. The need to naintain dykes and irrigation channels meant that Egypt became the first country in the world to have a national government. Measuring the flood and rebuilding field boundaries led to the development of mathematics. Because river transport was so easy, the Egyptians did not use wheeled vehicles, or domesticate the horse or camel, until much later.

Egyptian noblemen took their leisure on the river. Laundrymen and fishermen depended on it for their livelihood. Every Egyptian learned from earliest childhood to watch for crocodiles and hippopotami.

The peasants built their villages on man-made mounds above the flood. For most of them the time of flood, *Akhet*, was a time of rest. Those not drafted to mend the dykes or work on the pyramids, drank beer and enjoyed the holiday.

Every year, from June to September, melting snow pours down the mountains of Cush (Ethiopia) into Egypt. It washes down black mud, which fertilizes the soil for next year's harvest. It is the time of *Akhet*, the flood. The Egyptians believe that the Nile is a god, and that Khnum, the creator-god, causes the river to swell.

11

The Time of Drought

From October until February was the season of *Peret* (coming forth). The Egyptians ploughed, hoed and dug water channels. The Keeper of the Storeroom distributed seedcorn, which was sown by hand.

Farmers grew emmer (a type of wheat), barley, fruit and vegetables. They grew flax for linen cloth and papyrus reeds to make paper. They collected honey, because they had no sugar. Egyptians kept gazelles and cranes, as well as cattle, sheep, goats and pigs.

From February to June was the season of *Shemu* (drought), the time of the harvest. The labourers worked in 'hands' of five men under a *kherp* (the holder of the rod of discipline).

Back in the village the grain was trodden out on a threshing floor by oxen. Dung and dirt became mingled with the grain.

The peasants reap to the music of a flute. They pray to the goddess Isis as they work, because they believe that the cutting of the corn reminds her of how her husband was cut into pieces by his brother Seth (see page 49).

They cut the barley just below the ear (see above) to avoid carrying the useless straw back to the village. They let the ears fall to the ground, where they are gathered and loaded onto donkeys.

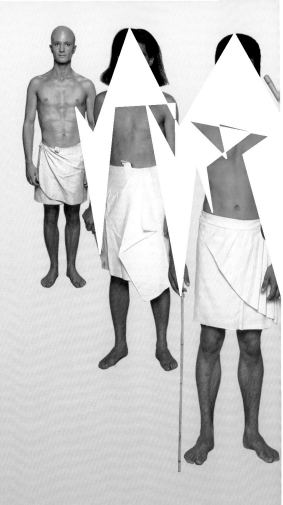

Egyptian Society

Chephren's highest officials were *imakhu* (friends of the pharaoh) and were usually members of the royal family. They led trade missions, commanded the army and acted as nomarchs (rulers of the nomes). The chief minister (the *tjaty*) was the Chief Judge, but he was also in charge of the Treasury and the House of the Granary (the Ministry of Agriculture). Sometimes, the pharaoh allowed an *imakhu* to build a tomb by the pyramids and to receive the food offerings which would help him live after death.

All government officials were scribes (educated men). Less important than the *imakhu* were the secretaries and sandal-bearers, and those who supervised the royal meals or worked as overseers on the pyramids. Many scribes served as priests in the hundreds of temples to the gods, or in the Mortuary Temples.

On a lower rung of society, the *hemutiu* – craftsmen such as weavers, sculptors, cobblers and jewellers – provided for the needs of the wealthy. Below them were the *mertu* (peasants), the majority of the population, who were given labouring jobs by the House of the Granary. There were no slaves in Egypt, but the *mertu* (on whose labour the whole of society depended) had no personal freedom. When the pharaoh gave land to a nobleman, the gift included the peasants who lived there. They had few possessions, and were beaten when they did not work hard enough.

Chephren, wearing a ceremonial gala skirt and a false beard, carries a crook and a flail, symbols of his power and concern for Egypt. Behind him stand (right to left) his son Mycerinus, a member of the royal family, a scribe (with his stick of authority), an overseer, a craftsman (*hemutiu*) and a peasant (*mertu*).

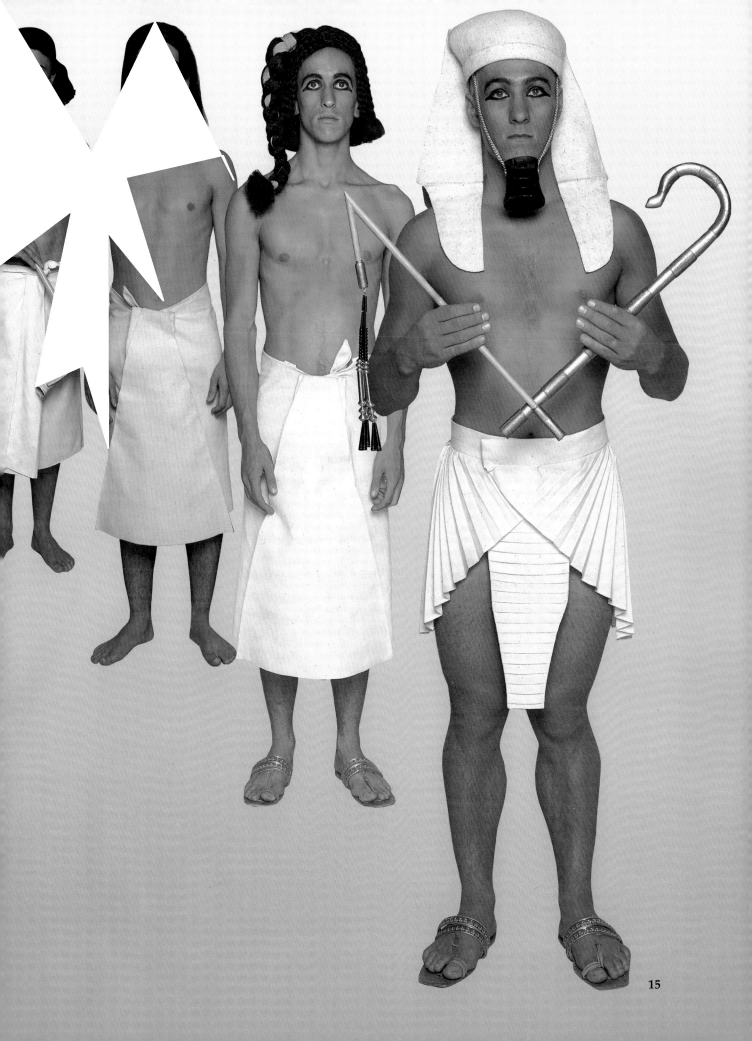

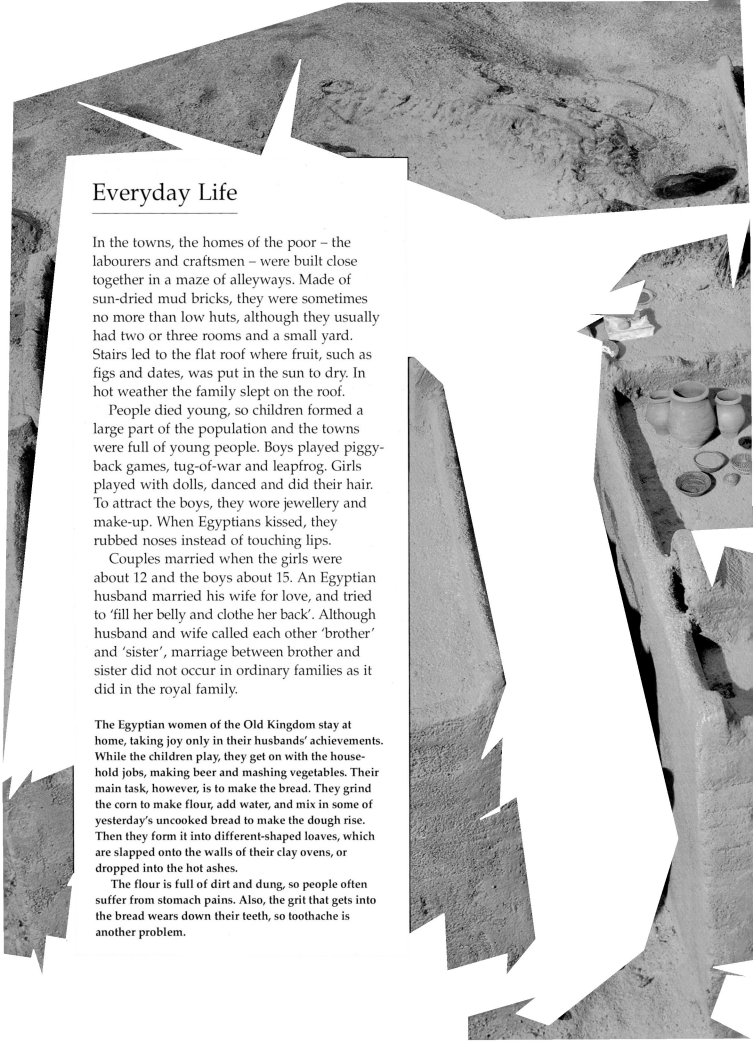

Everyday Life

In the towns, the homes of the poor – the labourers and craftsmen – were built close together in a maze of alleyways. Made of sun-dried mud bricks, they were sometimes no more than low huts, although they usually had two or three rooms and a small yard. Stairs led to the flat roof where fruit, such as figs and dates, was put in the sun to dry. In hot weather the family slept on the roof.

People died young, so children formed a large part of the population and the towns were full of young people. Boys played piggy-back games, tug-of-war and leapfrog. Girls played with dolls, danced and did their hair. To attract the boys, they wore jewellery and make-up. When Egyptians kissed, they rubbed noses instead of touching lips.

Couples married when the girls were about 12 and the boys about 15. An Egyptian husband married his wife for love, and tried to 'fill her belly and clothe her back'. Although husband and wife called each other 'brother' and 'sister', marriage between brother and sister did not occur in ordinary families as it did in the royal family.

The Egyptian women of the Old Kingdom stay at home, taking joy only in their husbands' achievements. While the children play, they get on with the household jobs, making beer and mashing vegetables. Their main task, however, is to make the bread. They grind the corn to make flour, add water, and mix in some of yesterday's uncooked bread to make the dough rise. Then they form it into different-shaped loaves, which are slapped onto the walls of their clay ovens, or dropped into the hot ashes.

The flour is full of dirt and dung, so people often suffer from stomach pains. Also, the grit that gets into the bread wears down their teeth, so toothache is another problem.

Make-up

Amongst the upper classes, the highlight of the day was the evening feast.

Egyptians, especially the men, took a great deal of trouble over dressing. Couples began to prepare themselves in the afternoon. They rubbed oil and perfumes into their skin, and shaved their heads and bodies with bronze razors. For health reasons, Egyptians often purged themselves, taking a laxative of senna and fruit to empty their bowels.

Although all Egyptians wore wigs, they did not want to go bald. To prevent this, they

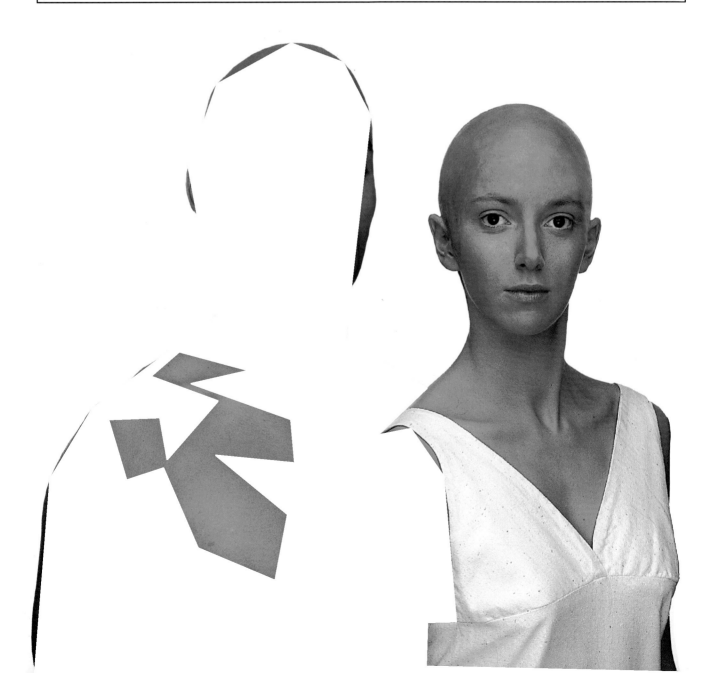

rubbed into their scalps substances such as gazelle dung and hippopotamus fat. The blood of a black bull, they believed, contained magic to prevent their hair going white.

It was important to smell nice, because body odour was a sign of sinfulness. Clothes were sprinkled with a perfume made from myrrh, frankincense and fragrant plants. Finally, a servant called the chief anointer placed a cone on top of each person's head. It was soaked with sweet-smelling ointment which, during the warm night, slowly melted over their hair. In this way they ensured that they smelt as nice at the end of the evening as at the beginning.

The ladies of Chephren's court chewed honey pills to make their breath sweet. They wore red lip salve and painted their toenails and fingernails red also. Round their eyes they used kohl, black eyeliner made from crushed lead ore, and blue eye shadow made from powdered copper ore.

Necklaces, bracelets and anklets completed their outfits.

Fashionable Egyptians put wigs on their shaved heads. They apply kohl to their eyes and eyebrows, blue eye shadow and lip salve, using a mixing palette and mirror (inset, left). The woman also wears an incense cone.

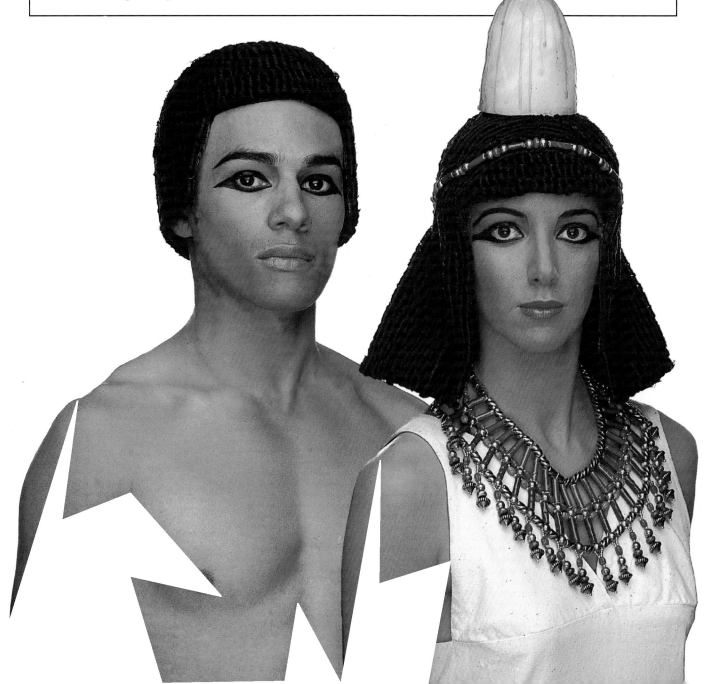

The Feast

In the Old Kingdom, court officials and their families lived with the pharaoh in the Palace of the White Wall. The richer officials, however, owned summer houses, where they could go to relax.

Feasts were held to celebrate all the main holy days, but often a wealthy man would order his servants to prepare a huge meal simply to entertain his friends. At such a feast his *ka* (spirit of generosity) would make him 'stretch out his arms in hospitality'. Beef, goat, antelope, goose and duck were offered to the guests by serving girls. All the dishes were cooked with imported herbs and spices.

Guests ate with their fingers. They drank a little wine, and four kinds of beer. They held lotus flowers to their noses, crushing them between their fingers to savour the scent.

Smell was important to the Egyptians; the drawing of a nose in Egyptian writing meant 'smell', 'taste', and also 'enjoy'. At a feast,

therefore, there was always a mixture of smells of perfumes, flowers, food and spices, which was heady and exotic.

Towards the end of the evening, singers, acrobats and magicians would entertain the guests. Girls performed slow dances, with elegant movements. Musicians played harps, lutes, zithers and the sistrum (a metal rattle) – although nobody knows what their music sounded like.

There were texts, written on papyrus, which told people how to behave at feasts. They advised guests to look at their food, so that no-one would think they were staring at them. A polite guest, they taught, spoke only when spoken to, and laughed when others laughed. 'This is how it is in Egypt,' explained one manual of good behaviour, 'and only a fool would complain about it.'

At a nobleman's feast, men and women sit apart. They stay seated all night, and do not join in the dancing or singing. They believe that mealtimes are precious to the gods and require good manners.

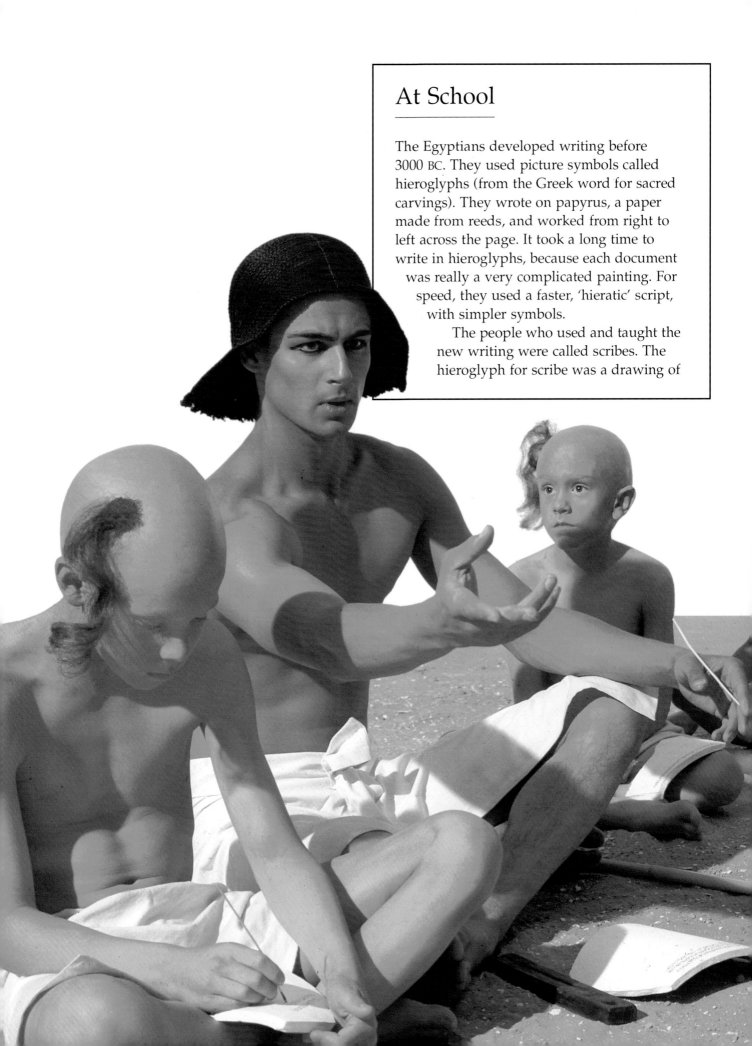

At School

The Egyptians developed writing before 3000 BC. They used picture symbols called hieroglyphs (from the Greek word for sacred carvings). They wrote on papyrus, a paper made from reeds, and worked from right to left across the page. It took a long time to write in hieroglyphs, because each document was really a very complicated painting. For speed, they used a faster, 'hieratic' script, with simpler symbols.

The people who used and taught the new writing were called scribes. The hieroglyph for scribe was a drawing of a paint palette with red and black paint, a water pot and a brush.

All Egyptian children went to school when they were four years old. At 12, they usually left. The boys began to learn their fathers' trade, while the girls helped their mothers in the house. The sons of officials went on studying for several years. Some girls also stayed on and became scribes, but in the Old Kingdom people mocked the writings of women.

Many careers were open to the scribes. They might work for the Army or the Treasury. They could go into medicine, the priesthood or architecture. Trainees were encouraged to work hard. The life of a scribe was better than most, one old document says. The scribe is his own boss, whereas 'the metal-smith works in the heat of the furnace. He stinks like rotten fish eggs.'

The scholars learn proverbs and stories by heart, and copy set texts onto specially prepared pieces of pottery and limestone slates.

They learn reading, writing and arithmetic, and older pupils study geography and history. They are not taught to think for themselves. Questioning and lack of respect are punished.

The master believes that a boy's ears are on his back – he only listens when you beat him.

The lessons are tediously boring. The pupils whisper and daydream, and long for noon, when their mothers will collect them, bringing a meal of bread and barley wine.

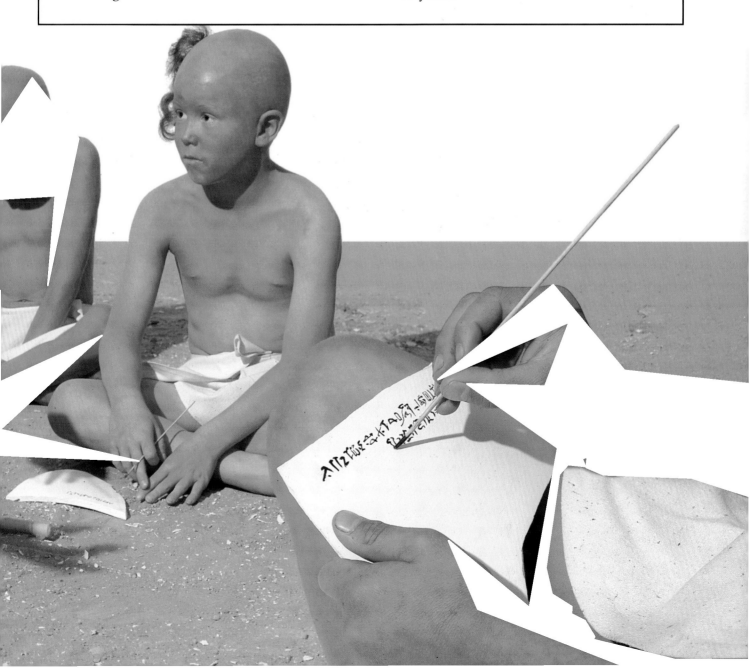

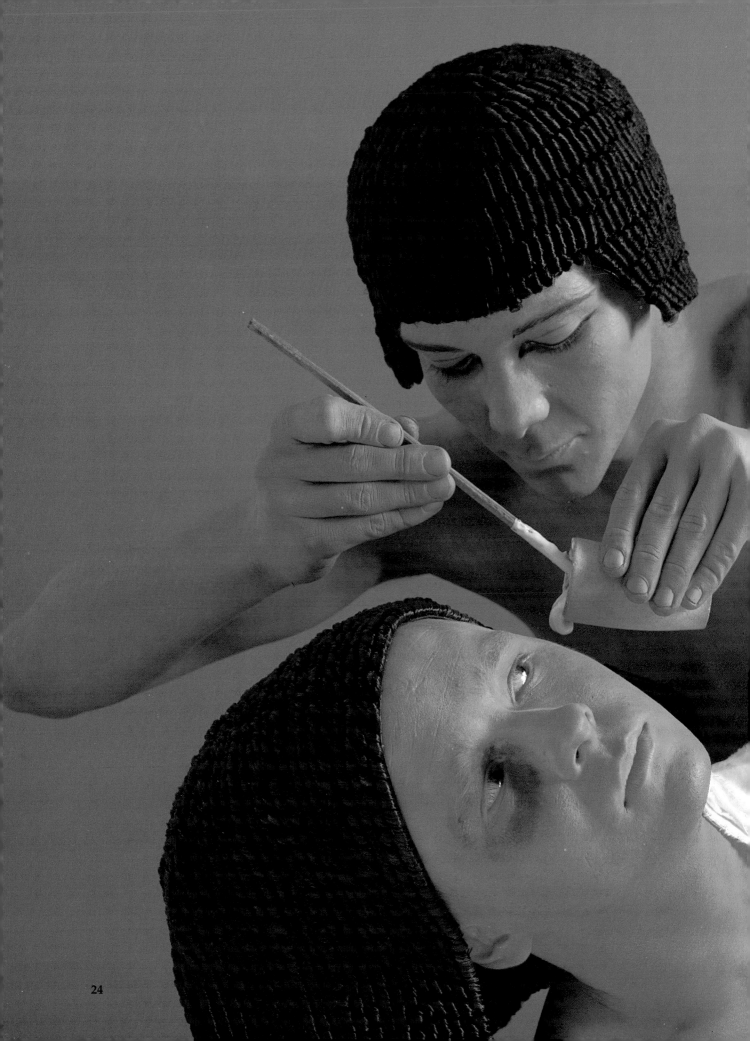

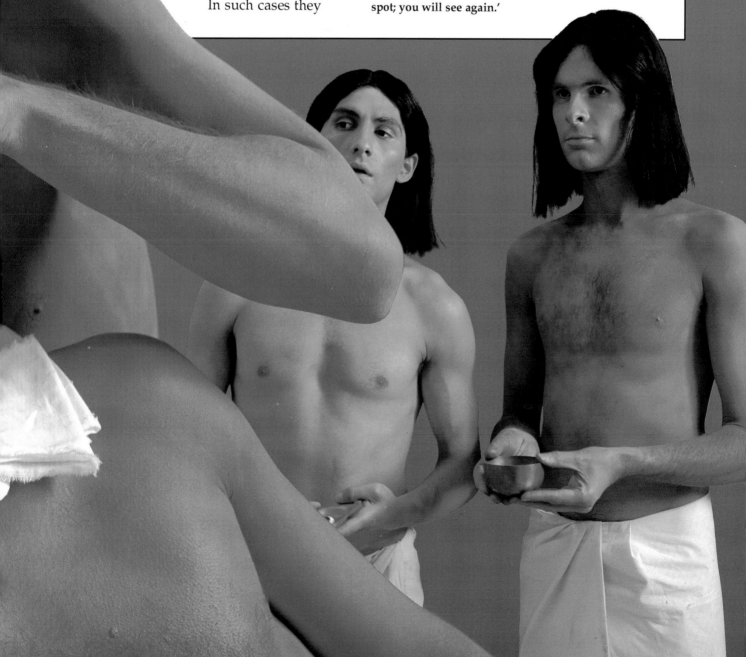

At the Doctor's

In the Old Kingdom, medicine was halfway between the magic of the witch-doctor and the science of the modern doctor.

Doctors had papyrus texts describing how to examine the patient and diagnose disease; they looked for symptoms such as 'blood like fried pig's blood'. They were expert at bandaging and first aid. Some of their medicines contained healing substances which are still used today. Often, however, doctors were powerless to relieve pain or prevent death. In such cases they

used magic cures. For example, the ointment for blindness contained a pig's eye, because the doctors believed it had the magical strength of sight. They also prescribed spells and charms of stinking herbs and fish as protection against the spirits.

A doctor might be asked to advise on how to get rid of fleas or even how to make clothes smell sweet. He was a wise man, who should know all the answers.

'You are going blind,' the doctor tells the nobleman, 'but this is a disease I can treat.' He takes a pig's eye, some red ochre and honey, and grinds them together. He pours the ointment into the patient's ear, then he recites a spell twice: 'I have applied this ointment to the trouble spot; you will see again.'

Hunting

Poor Egyptians hunted for food, trapping birds or fishing with different sorts of nets. Nobles hunted marsh birds with throw-sticks (rather like boomerangs) and fished with harpoons. Using these ancient weapons required great skill. Rich Egyptians also went out in small papyrus boats to hunt hippopotami with harpoons and ropes. It took a brave man to hunt the hippopotamus, which was very fierce and strong.

Other nobles went hunting in the desert. The minister in charge of the desert nome was also called Master of the Hunt. The nobles lassoed ibexes and antelopes, and reared them as domestic animals. Captured monkeys became ladies' pets, and baboons were used as guard animals in the markets. Nobles also chased leopards and lions with hunting dogs, and hoped to kill one of the legendary beasts of the desert: the sphinx, with the head of a man and the body of a lion, or a *sag*, half lion, half hawk.

Hunting was more than sport. In the legend of Horus (see page 49) the evil god Seth had hidden in the body of a hippopotamus. Seth was also thought to live in the animals of the desert. In killing these animals, the Egyptians repeated the victory of Horus over Seth, symbolizing the victory of civilization over disorder. Priests hunted lions to sacrifice to the Nile god, so he would make the flood rise again. The crocodile, Sebek, was a god in his own right.

As the hunters return home through the village with a catch of wildfowl, a young nobleman aims a throw-stick at a bird. In the background, peasants carry a sack of grain to be paid as tax.

Pharaoh's Decision

Chephren ruled Egypt like Re ruled over the gods. His authority was awesome. To touch the pharaoh's sceptre, even accidentally, carried the death penalty. A chief minister who was permitted to nose (kiss) the pharaoh's feet, instead of the ground before him, had been granted the highest honour.

The pharaoh controlled all trade. There was no private enterprise. He sent traders to Cush (Ethiopia), Punt (Somalia) and Byblos (Lebanon), miners to Sinai, and armies to Nubia (Sudan) and Libya.

Although Chephren was all-powerful, his life was restricted. He had to wake at dawn to be washed by the women of his harem (the court of his wives). Each day he had to offer food to his ancestors and take part in endless

religious services. Before each meal there were washings, mouth-rinsings and changing of clothes. He even ate according to strict ceremonies, because the meal was an offering to a god.

Each day the pharaoh examined the accounts and reports, dictated letters to his scribes, and issued commands. Sometimes he did not speak himself, but let officials speak for him. There were officials at the court called the Mouth, the Tongue and the Repeater.

Perhaps, in such a way, on one day in about 2555 BC, Pharaoh Chephren announced his decision to build a pyramid.

Mahnud Hotep, *imakhu*, architect and High Priest of the god Ptah (the god of craftsmen), is summoned before Chephren. He is formally appointed Great Chief of Works to the pyramid which is to be called 'Great is Chephren'.

Finding True North

The first task of the Great Chief of Works was to draw up the plans for the pyramid. It had to face towards the north. An old idea was that when the pharaoh died his soul would become a bird; with a lamp in its beak, it would fly off to become a star in the northern sky. The pyramid, therefore, had to be aligned with the Pole Star in the north.

The stars have changed their position in the skies over the centuries, so the star which the Egyptians called the Pole Star is the one we now call Alpha Draconis.

Egyptian priests studied the stars carefully, because the heavens were the home of the gods. They used astrology to calculate the 'lucky' and 'unlucky' days of the month, and also when the gods' festivals should fall. They had an accurate calendar by 4000 BC, a thousand years before the birth of Abraham. (The official Egyptian calendar was less successful. Lacking leap years, it was only right once every 1,460 years!)

When the priests had worked out the correct alignment of the pyramid, Chephren and Mahnud Hotep visited Giza on a 'lucky' day. They marked out the four corners of the site and put tools and charms underneath a foundation stone. These ceremonies were laid down in *The Book of Temple Building*, which they believed was written by Imhotep, the architect of the first pyramid.

The priest, who is called 'the watcher of time', carries a *bay* (palm stick). He takes a sighting on the Pole Star, lining up the star and the *bay* held by his servant. The line between them is true north. His measurements are so precise that the least accurate side of the pyramid is only one twelfth of one degree out of true.

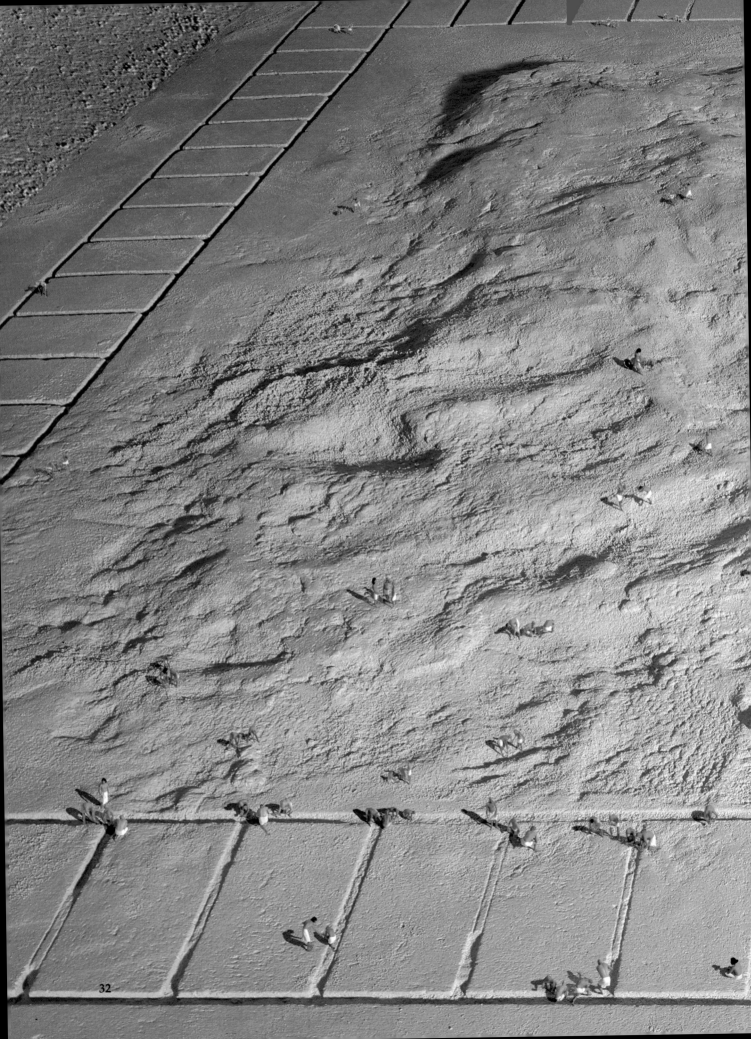

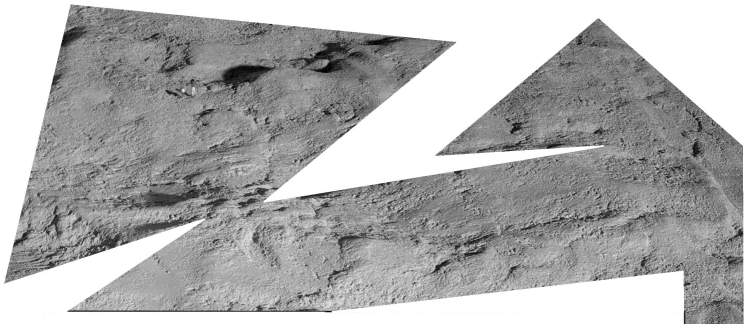

Levelling the Base

After the site had been prayed over, a team of workmen cleared the sand and set about levelling the rock beneath it.

Chephren's pyramid was built on a slope, and the base of the pyramid covered 11 acres. To level such a vast area they dug a system of trenches and filled them with water (see below). Water finds its own level, so when the planners marked the water line, it gave them a horizontal level over the whole area.

In many pyramids, only the rock around the edges was levelled. Inside, the builders left a rocky hill. This increased the structural strength of the pyramid.

Meanwhile, other workmen were cutting a short, sloping tunnel underneath the site. When they were 16 feet (5 metres) underground, they cut a small chamber into its east wall. A large granite stone was wedged into the tunnel ceiling, to be dropped down to seal the passage.

The masons then dug a second chamber in the centre of the base, 47 x 17 feet and 23 feet deep (15 x 5 x 7 metres). From here, another tunnel led to the edge of the site.

Nobody knows why the workmen built two underground chambers. There may have been a change of plan during construction, or perhaps the first tunnel was to confuse grave robbers.

Workmen level the rock to make a flat base for the pyramid. They have no machines or power tools, only hand tools made either of copper or a hard rock called dolerite. Because the copper tools are quickly worn down, a team of metal workers is kept busy sharpening old tools and making new ones.

At the Quarry

The stone blocks for the pyramid came from limestone quarries near Giza. Up to 1,000 men, divided into gangs, worked in the quarries. Each gang had a name. One of the stones in the Great Pyramid still has the tally mark of one of the gangs: 'Craftsmen Gang. How strong is the Crown of Cheops!'

The men cut down the sides of a block, using copper chisels. Then they chipped holes at the base and hammered in wedges of dry wood. When it was moistened, the wood expanded. This forced the block upwards, and caused the limestone to crack across underneath the block.

The gangs roughly squared the blocks with dolerite pounders. Large blocks were cut in half with a copper saw; wet sand poured into the groove acted as an abrasive and made cutting easier.

The casing stones, for the outside of the pyramid, were brought from quarries at Tura, on the far bank of the Nile. In the Tura quarries the highest quality stone lay deep in the hillside, so the men had to work in underground tunnels. The cut blocks were stored until the time of *Akhet*, when they were put on barges and rowed across the flooded river to the Giza pyramids.

Granite was quarried 500 miles (800 kilometres) south of Giza, at Aswan. The workers were frequently attacked by the neighbouring Nubians, so Chephren had to send soldiers to protect them. No-one went to Aswan by choice; they had to be conscripted (ordered).

Granite, which is stronger and harder than limestone, was used for pillars and roofing slabs in the pyramids. Some of the blocks of granite weighed as much as 50 tons, so bringing them such a distance was a major achievement.

Gangs of workmen haul blocks of stone towards the River Nile. Each block weighs nearly 3 tons. To move them the men have only rollers and levers.

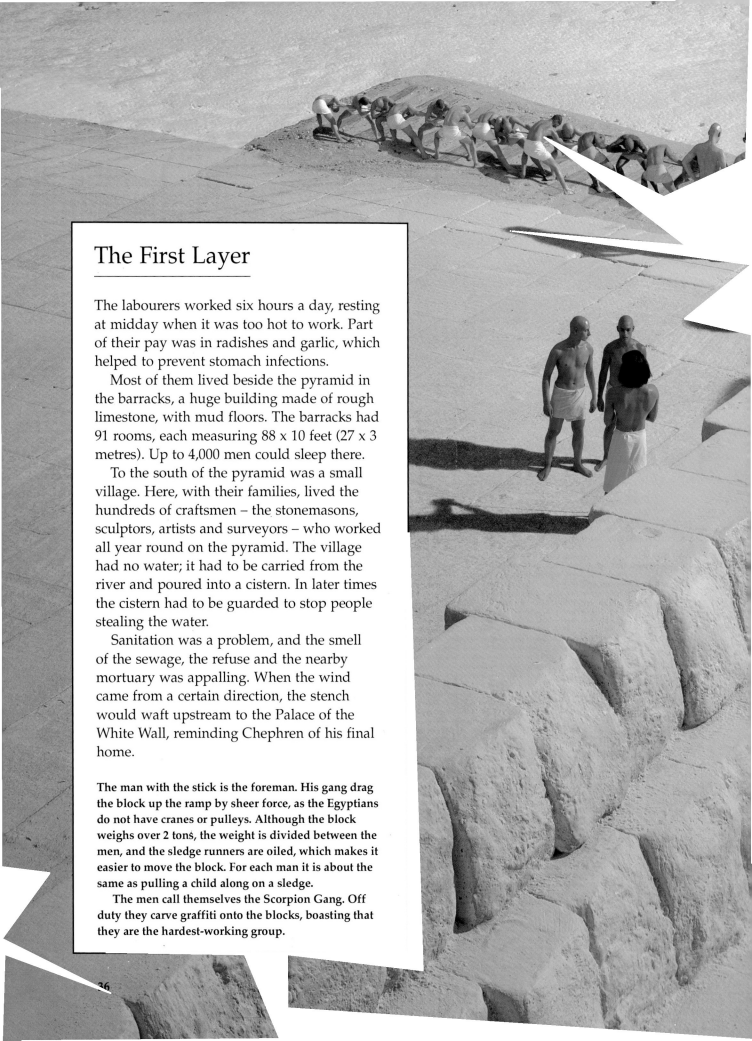

The First Layer

The labourers worked six hours a day, resting at midday when it was too hot to work. Part of their pay was in radishes and garlic, which helped to prevent stomach infections.

Most of them lived beside the pyramid in the barracks, a huge building made of rough limestone, with mud floors. The barracks had 91 rooms, each measuring 88 x 10 feet (27 x 3 metres). Up to 4,000 men could sleep there.

To the south of the pyramid was a small village. Here, with their families, lived the hundreds of craftsmen – the stonemasons, sculptors, artists and surveyors – who worked all year round on the pyramid. The village had no water; it had to be carried from the river and poured into a cistern. In later times the cistern had to be guarded to stop people stealing the water.

Sanitation was a problem, and the smell of the sewage, the refuse and the nearby mortuary was appalling. When the wind came from a certain direction, the stench would waft upstream to the Palace of the White Wall, reminding Chephren of his final home.

The man with the stick is the foreman. His gang drag the block up the ramp by sheer force, as the Egyptians do not have cranes or pulleys. Although the block weighs over 2 tons, the weight is divided between the men, and the sledge runners are oiled, which makes it easier to move the block. For each man it is about the same as pulling a child along on a sledge.

The men call themselves the Scorpion Gang. Off duty they carve graffiti onto the blocks, boasting that they are the hardest-working group.

Roofing the Burial Chamber

It took at least a month to lay the 30,000 blocks in the bottom layer of the pyramid. The workmen then prepared to position roofing slabs over the burial chamber.

Before they could do this, however, they had to lower the sarcophagus (stone coffin) into the chamber, as it was too large to be taken down the entrance tunnel. They filled the chamber with sand and dragged the sarcophagus onto the top. Then they scooped out the 1,000 tons of sand. As the sand level was lowered, the coffin descended into the chamber. Finally, it was manoeuvred into a hole which had been cut in the floor of the burial chamber.

To position the roof slabs, workmen again filled the room with sand. Using wooden rollers, they dragged the slabs across the first layer of the pyramid, then levered them onto the sand. One unfortunate gang then had to carry the 1,000 tons of sand out of the chamber along the entrance passage.

When it is finished, the weight of the entire pyramid will press down onto the roof slabs of the burial chamber, so they must be perfectly positioned. They are placed in a shallow, upside-down 'V', so that the downward pressure of the pyramid is diverted outwards onto the walls of the burial chamber.

Halfway There

Two thousand years after the time of Chephren, a Greek writer called Herodotus claimed that Chephren and Cheops were tyrants who enslaved the Egyptians and forced them to work on the pyramids. He claimed that '100,000 men laboured constantly, relieved every month by a fresh lot'.

It is now thought that, at most, only 8,000 men could have worked on the pyramid site at any one time. If more men had been involved, they would have got in each other's way. Nor were the workers unwilling slaves. Although they were made to work hard and the overseers were strict, they believed that the pharaoh was a god who protected the land, and that his eternal safety was everybody's concern. Also, they were paid in food at a time when the flooded fields could not produce crops.

Chephren's pyramid was 708 feet (216 metres) square at its base, and contained over two million blocks of stone. It is difficult to imagine the organization needed to build so large a structure.

Although thousands of peasants were

conscripted to do the unskilled labouring jobs, most of them were only available during the four months of *Akhet*. To build a pyramid in 20 years, a thousand blocks a day had to be put in place – three every minute. Also, as the pyramid grew, workers had to haul the blocks up long ramps before they could position them. Because of its shape, when the pyramid reached two-thirds of its final height only 4 per cent of the blocks remained to be dragged into position. The labourers, however, still had to pull about 80,000 blocks up the ramps.

Meanwhile, adding to the amount of work to be done, Chephren had ordered the construction of a smaller pyramid to the south of his own. Now almost totally destroyed, it was 65 feet (20 metres) square, and 42 feet (13 metres) high. It is sometimes called a 'queen's pyramid'. The entrance, however, is so small that an adult can hardly get into it, and it was probably built for religious reasons.

The overseer works late into the evening planning the next day's schedule. The pyramid is a marvel of Egyptian organization: over one hundred gangs will drag a continuous stream of stone blocks up the ramps to the summit. There must be no confusion.

Accident!

A pyramid may look simple to build, but the immense weight of the stone makes it very unstable. Imhotep, who designed the first pyramid, discovered how to spread the weight by constructing dozens of buttresses (vertical columns of blocks) inside the pyramid, 8 feet (2.5 metres) apart.

Even so, not all pyramids were successfully completed. Chephren's grandfather, Seneferu, seems to have built three pyramids. The pyramid at Meidum had buttresses only every 16 feet (5 metres) and it collapsed, perhaps after a rain storm. The roof of a chamber inside the Bent Pyramid cracked during building, forcing the builders to change the angle of the sides halfway up, to reduce its final height. The casing stones fell off the nearby Red Pyramid. These incidents make the successful construction of Chephren's pyramid all the more remarkable.

A moment's inattention turns a pyramid into a mountain as dangerous as any on earth. Every day, site doctors treat a succession of cut fingers, crushed toes and broken limbs. Only a lucky gang can boast that not one of its men has died during the building of the pyramid.

Royal Statues

Before the sculptors could begin work on a statue, various religious ceremonies had to be performed. Next, a draughtsman drew a grid of squares on the surface of the stone. Then on each side of the block he drew an outline of the pharaoh, from the front, sides and back. The knee was always drawn in the sixth square, the shoulders in the thirteenth. These rules, laid down in *The Book of the Artist*, explain why Egyptian art does not often look realistic.

The sculptors chipped back the profiles from each side until they met in the middle. Apprentices did the unskilled work at the beginning, and the Director of Sculptors added the finishing touches. Others worked on the reserve heads, which were placed in

the pyramid in case Chephren's body was lost or damaged.

Finally, the hieroglyphs of the names of Chephren were inscribed on the base of the statue. At this point, the Egyptians believed, the statue became Chephren. In later times wealthy Egyptians, rather than pay for their own statues, sometimes just chipped out the original name and added their own. It then became a statue of them.

Sculptors in the royal workshops carve the diorite statues of the pharaoh which will be placed in the Valley Temple of the pyramid, on the banks of the Nile. Some of the statues are finished, and await only the ceremony of the Opening of the Mouth to bring them to life.

The statues do not represent Chephren as he is – an old man about to die – but show the idealized face and body of a young man. The statues in the background have falcons carved on their shoulders, because the pharaoh is also the god Horus.

Casing and Finishing

Chephren's pyramid had 124 layers of stone. On top the builders placed a large granite capstone. With the capstone in place, the pyramid stood 471 feet (144 metres) high.

Working from the top of the pyramid to the bottom, workmen then positioned hundreds of casing blocks of Tura limestone. Although they have weathered over the centuries, in Chephren's time they were almost white. The lowest layer of casing stones was made of red Aswan granite. Nearby, sculptors carved a rocky outcrop into a giant sphinx. Its head had Chephren's features.

Over the years most of the casing blocks have been stolen for building stone; many were used to build the great mosque in Cairo in the sixteenth century. Only a few near the top of the pyramid remain in place.

Masons dress one of the limestone casing blocks. It must be correctly positioned to within a fraction of an inch.

When the masons have finished, priests, using plumb lines, will check that the angle of the slope is precisely correct (52.3 degrees). Labourers will then rub the casing blocks with polishing stones until they shine in the sun, and sculptors will inscribe them with hundreds of hieroglyphs, describing Chephren's entry into heaven to rule with the gods.

The Last Journey

The Egyptians believed that the dead went to the Kingdom of the West, a land ruled by the god Osiris. Many of the funeral ceremonies, therefore, were based on the story of Osiris.

According to the myth, Osiris was chopped into pieces by his brother Seth, who scattered his body all over Egypt. Isis, the wife of Osiris, searched for the body and collected the pieces together. The body was mummified, and each part was buried in a different place. By magic, Isis made each part turn into a whole body. Her son Horus touched the mouth of each body, so that it came to life. Horus then killed Seth. Although he was blinded in one eye during the battle, his sight was restored and he was made pharaoh of Egypt.

The death of the pharaoh was terrible for the Egyptians, because the pharaoh was the god Horus, who protected Egypt. When the pharaoh died, they felt as alone as a child in the desert without its father. Inside the palace men sat with their heads on their knees. Women let their dresses hang down off their shoulders. They wailed and sprinkled dirt on their heads. Professional mourners sang funeral songs.

It was important to carry out the religious ceremonies correctly. Without them Chephren could not be reborn, and the new pharaoh could not begin to reign.

Pharaoh Chephren has died and priests have performed the ceremony of 'searching' for the body, in the same way that Isis searched for Osiris. Now the dead pharaoh is carried from the Palace of the White Wall to the royal barge. The procession is led by the Lector Priest. He reads: 'The stars weep and the dead tremble, because pharaoh has risen to the horizon.'

The crown prince walks behind the priest. In the background, servants carry Chephren's possessions which he will need in the afterlife.

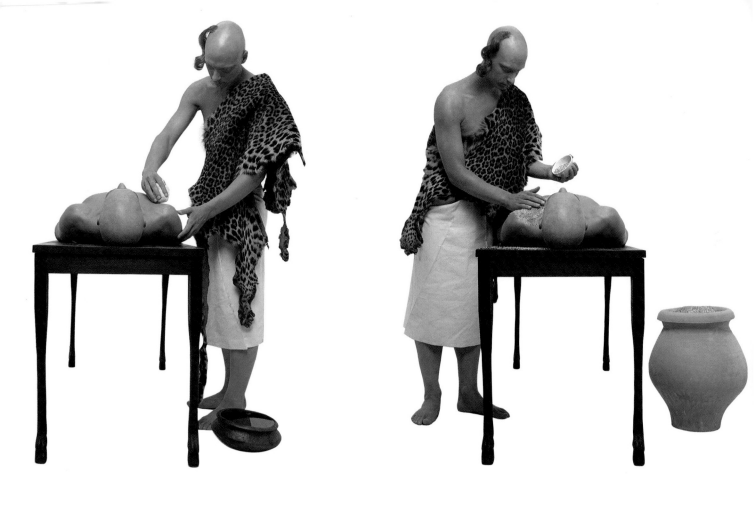

Mummification

Wealthy Egyptians were mummified after death, because they thought they would need their bodies in the afterlife.

Although poor people could not afford to be mummified, they were buried naked in the desert sand on their left sides, facing west. The sand dried out their bodies and preserved them just as effectively as the processes of mummification. Tools, jewellery and bowls of food were buried with them, showing that they hoped to go to the Kingdom of Osiris.

Chephren's corpse was laid on a funeral boat, under a canopy. A lamp burned in the bow. At either end stood two female mourners, representing the two goddesses, Isis and Nephthys. The body was taken down the Nile to Giza. The Egyptians believed that this short voyage represented the journey that the pharaoh would soon take across the marshes to heaven.

At Giza, the body was mummified. Mummification took about 70 days, and was carried out by special priests who belonged to the Guild of Embalmers. The ceremonies followed the myth of Osiris. The man who cut open the abdomen to remove the internal organs – the ripper – was stoned and driven away, perhaps because he reminded the onlookers of Seth, who chopped up the body of Osiris.

The body was washed, preserved in natron (a type of salt) and bandaged, just as Isis had done to preserve the body of Osiris. The stoppers of the four canopic jars (in which were put the liver, lungs, stomach and intestines) were carved into animal heads representing the four gods who, it was believed, protected the internal organs.

Priests wash the corpse in the *ibu* (purifying place), symbolizing its rebirth from the dead (above, far left). Then they rub the body with natron to dry and preserve the skin (above left).

The pharaoh's body is taken to the *wabt* (mummifying tent). Here the internal organs, which will rot quickly, are removed. They are dried out with natron crystals, wrapped in cloth soaked in liquid natron, and put into four canopic jars, to be buried near the pharaoh (above).

Next, the corpse is rubbed with perfumes and aromatic oils. Bandages, resins, natron, dried grass and sawdust are pushed into the stomach cavity to fill it out (above right).

After this, each part of the body is bandaged individually, as Isis had bandaged Osiris. Sometimes the linen bandages are cut to look like clothing, or even a false beard. Sweet-smelling resins are used to glue and stiffen them.

Great care is taken to avoid damaging the head. The priests try to make the face look as lifelike as possible, although the bandages covering it are painted green – the colour of Osiris' face (right).

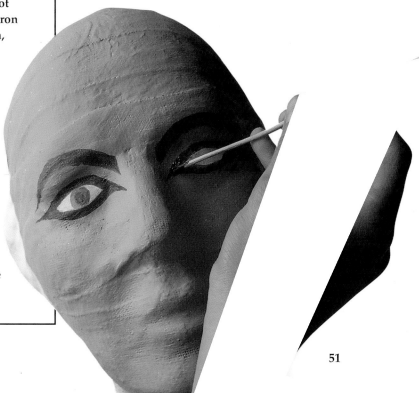

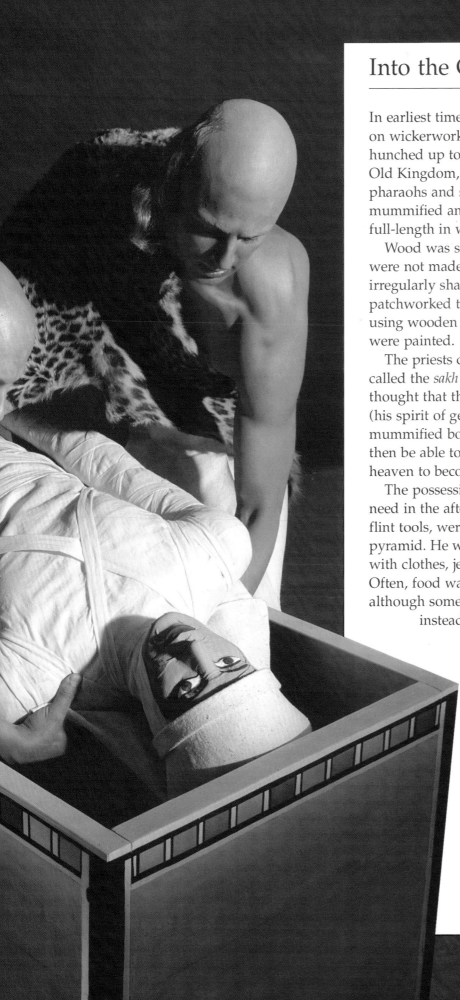

Into the Coffin

In earliest times, the Egyptians were buried on wickerwork trays, with their knees hunched up to their chests. During the Old Kingdom, however, the corpses of the pharaohs and some nobles began to be mummified and therefore had to be laid full-length in wooden coffins.

Wood was scarce in Egypt, so the coffins were not made of straight panels. The irregularly shaped pieces of wood were patchworked together, and fastened into place using wooden pegs. Sometimes the coffins were painted.

The priests conducted a religious ceremony, called the *sakh* (becoming a spirit). They thought that this made the pharaoh's *ka* (his spirit of generosity) return to live in his mummified body. The dead pharaoh would then be able to come back to life and go to heaven to become a god.

The possessions that the pharaoh would need in the afterlife, such as furniture and flint tools, were put in a storeroom in the pyramid. He would probably also be supplied with clothes, jewellery and scented cones. Often, food was put in the tomb as well, although sometimes stone models were used instead. The Egyptians believed that just as the pharaoh's mummy came to life by magic, by magic he would be able to take in the goodness of the food.

Priests lower the mummy into its wooden coffin. The body will be placed on its left side. The names and titles of Pharaoh Chephren are inscribed on the coffin. Inside, there is a list of the food and drink that the pharaoh expects to be left for him in the Mortuary Temple beside the pyramid.

Opening the Mouth

The doorways of the Valley Temple were inscribed with Chephren's name and titles. Sunlight reflected off the white alabaster floor, creating an unearthly, holy atmosphere. In the temple stood 23 statues of Pharaoh Chephren, one for each part of his body. The statues were 'brought to life' by the Opening of the Mouth ceremony. The Egyptians believed that this gave the dead pharaoh's *ka* 23 other resting places, in addition to the mummified body.

After this ceremony, Chephren's coffin was taken up a covered ramp to the Mortuary Temple beside the pyramid. The ramp was a marvellous building, a quarter of a mile (400 metres) long, lit by slits in the roof. In the temple a bull was killed and prayers were said. The priests believed that the strength of the bull would help Chephren rise from the dead.

Finally, Chephren's coffin was carried along the tunnel to the burial chamber inside the pyramid, and lowered into the stone sarcophagus. The lid of the sarcophagus was sealed in place. Only then could the crown prince take the throne and the title of pharaoh.

The Opening of the Mouth ceremony gives life to the statue of Pharaoh Chephren. It copies the ways in which Horus and Isis restored Osiris to life.

The ceremony is performed by priests, including the crown prince (right), the son of the dead pharaoh.

The priests sprinkle the statue with water, waft incense over it and offer sacrifice. They touch its mouth with a chisel and a tool called an adze. Then they rub milk on its lips and dress it in royal clothes.

The Pharaoh at Rest

The Egyptians had many different ideas about what happened to Chephren when his mummified body was placed in the pyramid.

According to the priests of Re, the pharaoh went to heaven, to rule with Re in the kingdom of the gods. Texts written in certain pyramids describe his arrival: 'The bolts of the doors fly open. He eats the gods for his meals.' In heaven he became one of the *imakhu* of Re, and helped Re take the sun across the sky.

According to the priests of Osiris, the pharaoh went to rule the Kingdom of the West. There he became Osiris. As the pharaoh, Chephren had represented the god Horus. After his death, however, his son ruled in Egypt. Chephren was now the father of the pharaoh-Horus, and the father of Horus was Osiris.

As Osiris, Chephren used his divine power to defend Egypt and the new pharaoh. This explains why Chephren's pyramid was so massive. It was a fortress designed to keep his mummified body safe, so that he could continue to protect Egypt.

It failed in its task. When an Italian, Giovanni Belzoni, discovered the entrance to the pyramid in 1818, he found the storeroom empty and the tomb open. The polished granite lid of the sarcophagus lay broken on the floor. Chephren's body had been removed.

The crown prince and the priests leave the burial chamber, and seal the tunnel leading to it. They have even brushed their footprints off the floor. Above, thousands of tons of masonry protect Chephren's body. In the royal chamber of Chephren's pyramid all is quiet.

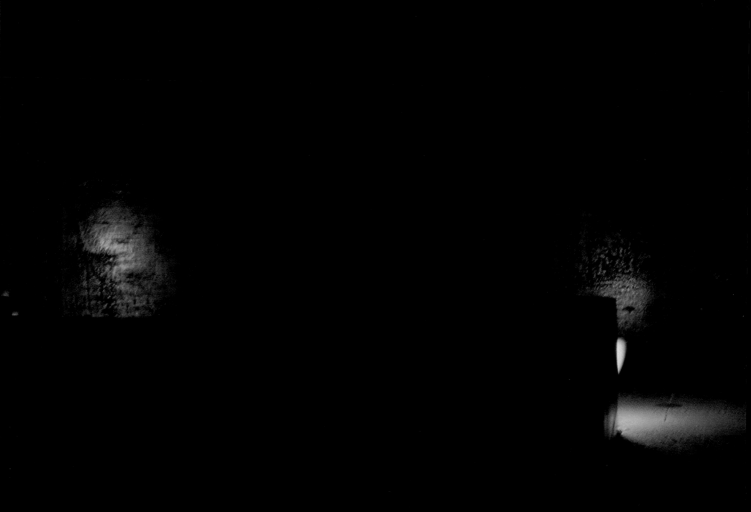

Offerings to the Dead

To ensure Chephren's eternal safety, priests constantly performed religious ceremonies at the Mortuary Temple. Their most important task was to provide food for his *ka*; Chephren did not want to be like the neglected dead, who went hungry and were forced to eat their own dung. He set up farms to support his priests and to provide the food offerings. The *ka* priests were forbidden to do any other work.

It is a strange fact that the most flourishing business in the Old Kingdom was the business of death. A pharaoh building a pyramid was the biggest customer of the country's building, quarrying and shipping industries. He was also the greatest patron of painters and sculptors. Building a pyramid developed the skills of astronomers, architects and mathematicians. Conscripting workers and collecting taxes to pay for the building work kept thousands of civil servants busy. Most Egyptian men worked on a pyramid at some time. Some worked there all their lives.

The vast scale of all this activity strained the Egyptian economy. Every pharaoh and nobleman who built a tomb added to the problem. Ministering to the dead used up so much wealth, land and food that the care of the dead harmed the living.

To become pure, the priest has washed three times, shaved his body, and put on clean, white linen clothes. He brings offerings of food for Chephren, placing them before a false door carved in the stone wall of the Mortuary Temple. Chephren's *ka*, he believes, will come out to eat the offering.

The Boat Pits

Even though Chephren had been buried, work on the pyramids did not stop. It was the duty of Chephren's son, Mycerinus, to complete the buildings around his father's pyramid, while he started to build his own. A pyramid complex was usually too large an undertaking to be completed during the reign of one pharaoh.

It is probable that neither the Valley Temple nor the Mortuary Temple were finished when Chephren died. Craftsmen had yet to decorate the covered way that led between them. According to Herodotus, who visited Giza in about 450 BC, the walls were covered with painted reliefs. Perhaps they showed the glories of Chephren's reign, or scenes from everyday life.

Beside the Mortuary Temple labourers dug six large boat pits. Similar pits have been found near a number of Egyptian graves. One was discovered as recently as 1954, near the Great Pyramid of Cheops. It was covered by 41 stone sleepers, cemented with pink mortar. The archaeologists could smell incense, 4,500 years old. In the pit was the pharaoh's royal boat. It had been dismantled into 1,224 pieces, but was preserved well enough to be rebuilt.

Shipwrights dismantle the funeral boat which carried Chephren's body to Giza. The boat is made of cedar wood from Byblos (Lebanon). The planks are tied together with rope. Each is marked with a sign to show where it belonged – port, starboard, fore or aft. The oars are left in place and the ship faces west, ready to carry the pharaoh to the Kingdom of Osiris.

The boat is laid in one of the six boat pits. This pit has been given a coating of plaster to make it airtight. Soon, stonemasons will drag large stone blocks into position to cover it.

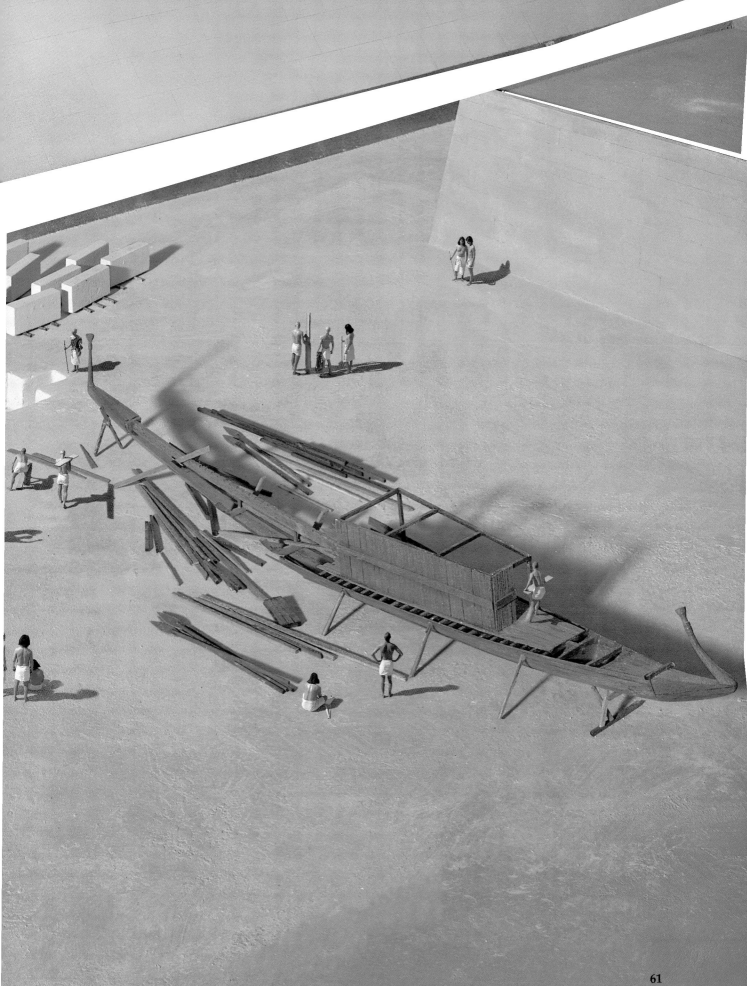

61

How Do We Know?

The end of the ancient Egyptians

The ancient Egyptian civilization lasted for two thousand years after the end of the Old Kingdom. Then, in 332 BC, Egypt was conquered by the Greeks. Slowly, the ancient Egyptian culture and writing began to disappear. In AD 391 the Romans closed most of the Egyptian temples, and people lost the ability to read hieroglyphs altogether.

Jewish, Greek and Roman sources

For a long time all that was known about the ancient Egyptians was what the Jews and Greeks had written about them.

The Jewish stories of Joseph and Moses contain descriptions of life in Egypt, although they are biased against the Egyptians. It is now known that the Egyptians told their own versions of these stories.

The Greeks, and later the Romans, laughed at the Egyptians, who worshipped eels instead of eating them and went to war because of a quarrel over a holy crocodile.

Their books, however, give a lot of information about the Egyptians. Manetho, an Egyptian who lived in Roman times, wrote a list of the pharaohs in 31 dynasties which is still used today. Herodotus visited and described Egypt in about 450 BC, although historians have to remember that he was writing 2,000 years after Chephren, and that he spiced his books with titbits of scandal.

Misunderstandings

For many years, therefore, little was known about the pyramids. People believed that they were observatories, or granaries built by Joseph for the pharaoh. It was also claimed that they were part of an attempt to measure the earth.

Even today, people put forward extraordinary theories about the pyramids – for example, that they were built by travellers from outer space, or that a pyramid's shape can sharpen razors, as well as preserve dead bodies.

Hieroglyphs and archaeology

The most reliable information about the ancient Egyptians, however, comes from the Egyptians themselves – from their writings and their monuments.

In 1799 a soldier serving with Napoleon found the Rosetta Stone. It had the same

inscription written three times: in Greek, in demotic (another form of Egyptian writing), and in hieroglyphs. The name Ptolmis occurred a number of times in the text, and scholars realized that the hieroglyphs which made up the name were always outlined by an oval cartouche. In 1822, by comparing the letters with those in the cartouche of Queen Kliopadrat (Cleopatra), a Frenchman called Jean François Champollion worked out the meaning of the hieroglyphs. He was the first person to understand them since AD 400.

It was soon realized that the Coptic language (which was still spoken in some Egyptian monasteries) was similar to the

language that had been spoken by the ancient Egyptians, 5,000 years before. Today, historians can read texts written by scribes who lived during Chephren's reign. They can read, for example, how an *imakhu* had become the *tjaty*; what was brought back from an expedition to Nubia (Sudan); and what medicines were prescribed by Egyptian doctors. Hundreds of spells carved on the walls of certain pyramids – the pyramid texts – show what Egyptians believed would happen to the pharaoh in the afterlife.

Meanwhile, archaeologists had begun to study the tombs, temples and other remains of the ancient Egyptians. One famous archaeologist, W.M.F. Petrie (1853–1942), excavated dozens of sites all over Egypt, working at night in nothing but his pink underwear.

Interpretation and mistakes

There are many things, nevertheless, which we still do not know. Nobody, for instance, knows where mummification took place in the Old Kingdom, or exactly how a pyramid

was built. The pictures in this book follow an American theory of a spiral of ramps around the pyramid. Other historians think that there was just one huge ramp leading up to the top of the pyramid. Neither ramp theory is very convincing. A single ramp would have been over a mile long, and a bigger building job than the pyramid itself!

Translators and archaeologists can give us the facts about what has survived from the past, but the historian has to interpret those facts to learn what life was like. It would be easy, for instance, to decide that all Egyptians were obsessed by death and worked for the government, but this is unlikely to be true. We just get this impression because most information comes from the graves of rich government officials. A historian must study the sources, and then form a personal opinion.

Perhaps, one day, you too will make a special study of Egypt, and develop opinions of your own.

Index